THE BOOK OF
ECHO SONGS

I'll Sing After You

REVISED EDITION

Compiled by John M. Feierabend

GIA PUBLICATIONS, INC. · CHICAGO

Also by John M. Feierabend, published by GIA Publications, Inc.:
The Book of Fingerplays and Action Songs
The Book of Movement Exploration
The Book of Pitch Exploration
The Book of Call and Response
The Book of Children's SongTales
The Book of Beginning Circle Games
The Book of Songs and Rhymes with Beat Motions

For infants and toddlers:
The Book of Lullabies
The Book of Wiggles and Tickles
The Book of Simple Songs and Circles
The Book of Bounces
The Book of Tapping and Clapping

On Compact Disc for infants and toddlers:
'Round and 'Round the Garden: Music in My First Year!
Ride Away on Your Horses: Music, Now I'm One!
Frog in the Meadow: Music, Now I'm Two!

On DVD and Compact Disc by Peggy Lyman and John M. Feierabend:
Move It! Expressive Movements with Classical Music
Move It 2! Expressive Movements with Classical Music

G-5277
The Book of Echo Songs (Revised Edition)
Compiled by John M. Feierabend
www.giamusic.com/feierabend

Copyright © 2020, 2003
GIA Publications, Inc.
7404 S. Mason Avenue
Chicago, IL 60638

Table of Contents

Introduction

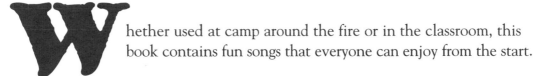hether used at camp around the fire or in the classroom, this book contains fun songs that everyone can enjoy from the start.

Unlike most songs, which take time to master, these Echo Songs enable everyone to sing immediately.

In an Echo Song, the leader sings a phrase and the group sings the phrase back. With one phrase, a cluster of disparate individuals transforms itself into a community bound by shared experience.

Songs such as these have existed for generations in work settings, be it in the fields or on ships. They helped pass the time and keep the workers in sync with each other.

All of the Echo Songs in this book have withstood the test of time, having been passed down from generation to generation.

Everyone loves Echo Songs because they are so accessible and fun.

Enjoy!

John M. Feierabend

ECHO SONGS

Alabama Bound

Leader: Group:

I'm Al - a - ba - ma bound,   I'm Al - a - ba - ma bound,

I'm Al - a - ba - ma bound,   I'm Al - a - ba - ma bound,

Leader:

and   if   the   train   don't   stop   and   turn   a -

Group:

round, I'm Al - a - ba - ma bound,   I'm Al - a - ba - ma bound.

All Hid

Leader: All hid, Group: All hid,

All hid, All hid,

Leader: five, ten, fif - teen, twen - ty,

twen - ty - five, thir - ty, thir - ty - five, for - ty,
for - ty - five, fif - ty, fif - ty - five, six - ty,
six - ty - five, sev'n - ty, sev'n - ty - five, eigh - ty,
eigh - ty - five, nine - ty, nine - ty - five, a hundred.

Here I come, read - y or not.

All Night Long

the book of echo songs

come
some - thing's wrong   on   the

If the train don't   come

road.

some - thing's wrong   on   the   road.

Chorus

Verse 2

If I live...and don't get killed...
I'll make my home...in Louisville...

Chorus

Verse 3

I'd rather be dead ...and in my grave...
Than in this old town...treated this
way...

Chorus

Verse 4

If anyone asks you...who wrote this
song...
Tell 'em 'twas me, and I sing it all
night long...

Banks of the Ohio

I asked my love, to take a walk,

I asked my love, to take a

To take a walk, just a lit - tle

walk, To take a walk,

walk, Down be - side,

just a lit - tle walk, Down be -

where the wa - ters flow, Down by the

side, where the wa - ters flow,

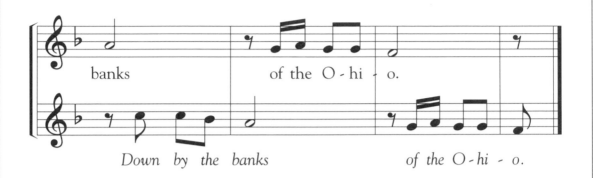

While the following verses tell the whole story, you may wish to use only the first verse with young children.

Refrain

Oh, darling say...that you'll be mine...
In no other's arms...entwine...
Down beside...where the waters
   flow...
Down by the banks...of the Ohio...

Bill Grogen's Goat

Leader: Group:

There was a man, *There was a man,*

Now please take note, *Now please take note,*

There was a man, *There was a man,*

Who had a goat. *Who had a goat.*

He loved that goat, *He loved that goat,*

In - deed he did, *In - deed he did,*

the book of echo songs

He loved that goat, *He loved that goat,*

Just like a kid, *Just like a kid.*

Verse 2

One day that goat...
  Felt frisk and fine...
Ate three red shirts...
  Right off the line...
The man, he grabbed....
  Him by the back...
And tied him to...
  The railroad track...

Verse 3

Now, when that train...
  Came into sight...
That goat grew pale...
  And green with fright...
He heaved a sigh...
  As if in pain...
Coughed up those shirts...
  And flagged the train...

Bury Me Not

Leader: "Oh, bur-y me not, on the lone prai-

Group: "Oh, bur-y me not,

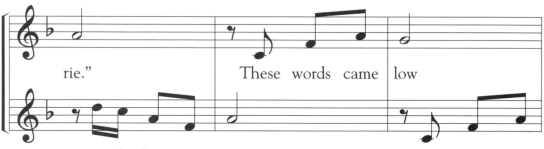

rie." These words came low

on the lone prai-rie." These words came

and mourn-ful-ly, From the pal-lid

low and mourn-ful-ly,

lips of a youth who lay,

From the pal-lid lips of a youth who

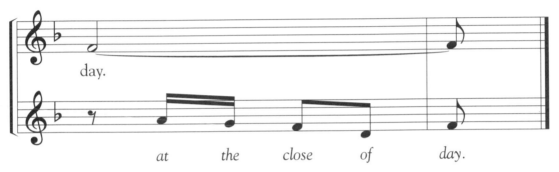

Verse 2

"Oh, bury me not...
   on the lone prairie...
Where the coyotes howl...
   and the wind blows free...
In a narrow grave...
   just six by three...
Oh, bury me not...
   on the lone prairie..."

Verse 3

"Oh, bury me not..."
   and his voice failed there...
But we took no heed...
   to his dying prayer...

In a narrow grave...
   just six by three. ..
We buried him there...
   on the lone prairie...

Verse 4

Yes, we buried him there...
   on the lone prairie...
Where the old night owl...
   hoots mournfully...
And the blizzard howls...
   and the wind blows free...
O'er that lonely grave...
   on the lone prairie...

Caney Mi Macaro *Cuban*

Leader:
Ca - ney mi ma - ca - ro, Ca - ney mi ma - ca - ro. (Group:)

Ca - ney mi ma - ca - ro, Ca - ney mi ma - ca - ro.

Ca - ney mi ma - ca - ro, Ca - ney mi ma - ca - ro.

Ca - ney mi ma - ca - ro, Ca - ney mi ma - ca - ro.

Ca - ney mi ma - ca - ro, Ca - ney mi ma - ca - ro.

Ca - ney mi ma - ca - ro, Ca - ney mi ma - ca - ro.

Translation

Though this song's lyrics have no specific meaning, the word *caney* means "hut."

Charlie Over the Ocean

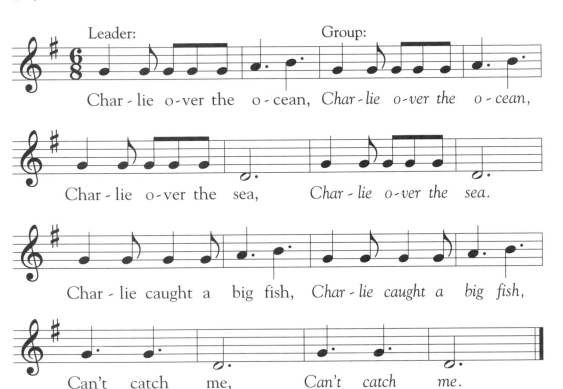

Leader:
Char - lie o - ver the o - cean,

Group:
Char - lie o - ver the o - cean,

Char - lie o - ver the sea,

Char - lie o - ver the sea.

Char - lie caught a big fish, Char - lie caught a big fish,

Can't catch me, Can't catch me.

Motions

One child walks around the outside of the circle of children. At the end of the song that child taps another child on the shoulder and then runs around the circle in an attempt to arrive at the space the other child left before the other child can catch him/her.

The leader part should be sung by the child who is walking around the circle.

Come All Ye Fair Ladies

Verse 2

They'll tell you... some loving story...
And they'll declare... their love is true...
Straight way they'll go... and court some
  other...
And that's the love... they have for you...

Verse 3

O, don't you remember... our days of
  courtin'...
When your head lay... upon my breast...?
You could make me believe... by the
  falling of your arm....
That the sun... rose in the west...

Verse 4

If I had known... before I courted...
That love had been... so hard to win...

I'd have locked my heart... in a box of
  gold...
And fastened it up... with a silver
  pin...

Verse 5

I wish I were... a little sparrow...
And I had wings... and I could fly...
I'd fly away... to my false true lover...
And when he would speak... I would
  deny...

Verse 6

But I am not... a little sparrow...
I have no wings... nor can I fly...
I will sit right down... in grief and
  sorrow...
And try to pass... my troubles by...

Come Along

Leader: Come a-long, Sing a song, Fol-low

Group: Come a-long, Sing a song,

me; It is eas-y as you see. Eve-ry

Fol-low me; It is eas-y as you

day, In this way, Just re-

see. Eve-ry day, In this way,

peat,   'Til the tune's com - plete.

Just re - peat,   *'Til the tune's com - plete.*

The Deacon Went Down

Leader: Group:

Oh, the Dea-con went down, *Oh, the Dea-con went down,*

In the cel-lar to pray, *In the cel-lar to pray,*

He fell a - sleep, *He fell a - sleep,*

And he stayed all day, *And he stayed all day.*

All:

Oh, the Dea-con went down in the cel-lar to

pray, He fell a - sleep and he stayed all

day,   I   ain't   a - gon - na   grieve   my

Lord   no   more.

Verse 2

I grieved my Lord....
From day to day...
I left the straight...
And narrow way...
(All) I grieved my Lord from day to day,
      I left the straight and narrow way,
      I ain't a-gonna grieve my Lord no more.

Verse 3

An' you can't get to heaven...
On a pair of skates...
'Cause you'll roll right past...
Those pearly gates...
(All) An' you can't get to heaven on a pair of skates,
      'Cause you'll roll right past those pearly gates,
      I ain't a-gonna grieve my Lord no more.

Verse 4

If you get to heaven...Before I do...
Just bore a hole...And pull me through...
(All) If you get to heaven before I do,
      Just bore a hole and pull me through,
      I ain't a-gonna grieve my Lord no more.

Down By the Bay

Down   by   the   bay,   *Down   by   the   bay,*

Where the wa-ter-mel-ons grow, *Where the wa-ter-mel-ons grow,*

Back   to   my   home, *Back   to   my   home,*

I   dare   not   go,   *I   dare   not   go,*

For   if   I   do,   *For   if   I   do,*

My   moth-er would   say,   *My   moth-er would   say,*

"Did you ev-er see a bear comb-ing his hair,

Down by the bay."

Verse 2

Solo: Did you ever see llamas,
wearing pajamas...

Verse 3

Solo: Did you ever see a whale,
with a polka-dotted tail...

Verse 4

Solo: Did you ever see a bee,
with a sunburned knee...

Verse 5

Solo: Did you ever see a goose,
kissing a moose...

make up additional verses

Ev'ry Night

Leader: Ev-'ry night, when the sun goes in,

Group: Ev-'ry night, when the sun goes

Ev-'ry night when the sun goes

in, Ev-'ry night

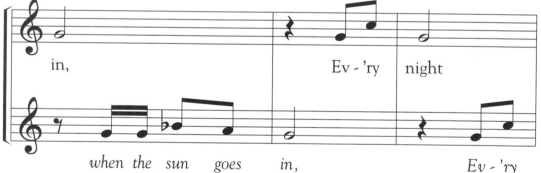

in, Ev-'ry night

when the sun goes in, Ev-'ry

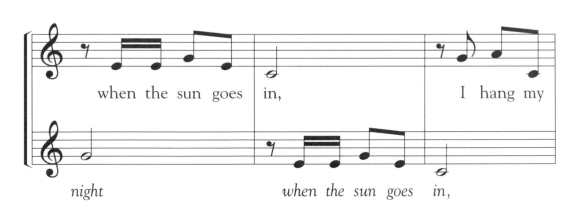

when the sun goes in,

I hang my

night

when the sun goes in,

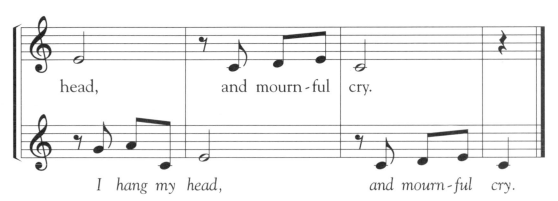

head,

and mourn-ful cry.

I hang my head,

and mourn-ful cry.

Verse 2

If the stars...in the sky won't shine...
   (*3 times*)
I hang my head...and mournful cry...

Verse 3

If the moon...hides behind a cloud...
   (*3 times*)
I hang my head...and mournful cry...

Flea! Fly!

Flea!*   Fly!

Flea fly!   Flea fly flo!

Vis - tay, Cu - ma la - da,

cu - ma la - da, cu - ma -la vis - tay.

Oh, no no no not the vis - tay,

Vis - tay, En - ney Mee - ney

des - a - mee - ney oo watch - a wah.

Hec - ta min - i - ca   zol - a ween - ie   oo watch - a   wah.

Bee   bid - dle de   oap boap   boap boap um - boap boap

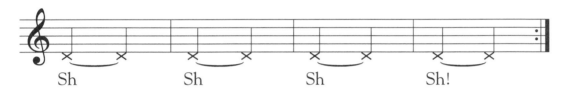

Sh   Sh   Sh   Sh!

*The Leader sings each segment and the
Group repeats each segment. Maintain
a tap-clap pattern throughout.*

Freedom Land

Leader: I'm on my way   to the free-dom

Group: *I'm on my way*

land.   I'm on my way

to the free-dom land.   *I'm on my*

to the free-dom land.   I'm on my

way   *to the free-dom land.*

Hang About

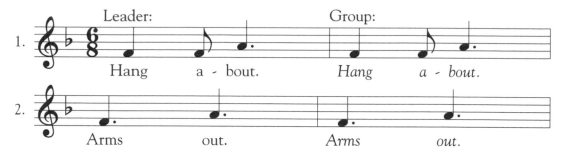

1. Leader: Hang a - bout. Group: Hang a - bout.

2. Arms out. Arms out.

All chant: Dum de da, dum, de, da, dum de da da da (Swing arms back and forth.)

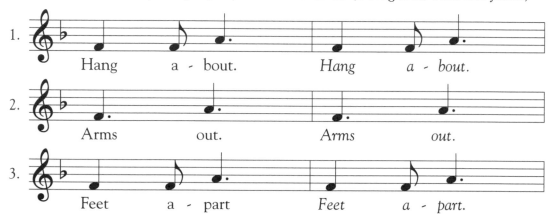

1. Hang a - bout. Hang a - bout.

2. Arms out. Arms out.

3. Feet a - part Feet a - part.

All chant: Dum de da, dum, de, da, dum de da da da (Swing arms back and forth.)

4. Knees to - geth - er. Knees to - geth - er.

Do 1, 2, 3 then 4 followed by the chant: Dum de da, dum, de, da, dum de da da da

5. Bot - tom's out. Bot - tom's out.

Do 1, 2, 3, 4 then 5 followed by the chant: Dum de da, dum, de, da, dum de da da da

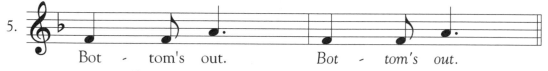

6. Tongue's out. Tongue's out.

Do 1, 2, 3, 4, 5 then 6 followed by the chant with tongue still out:
Dum de da, dum, de, da, dum de da da da

He, He, Wanna Wawate *Native American, Dakota people*

Leader:

He, he, wan - na wa - wa - te.

Group:

He, he, wan - na wa - wa - te.

Leader:

Wan - na wa - tinn - te,

Group:

Wan - na wa - tinn - te!

General translation

Joyously we feast, eating pemmican.
*(Pemmican is a Native American dish
made of dried buffalo meat pounded with
tallow, wild-cherries, and spices.)*

I Met a Bear

The oth - er day, *The oth - er day,*

I met a bear, *I met a bear,*

Out in the woods, *Out in the woods,*

A - way out there, *A - way out there,*

The oth - er day I met a bear,

Out in the woods a - way out there.

Verse 2

I looked at him...he looked at me...
I sized up him...he sized up me...
(All) I looked at him, he looked at me,
    I sized him up, he sized up me.

Verse 3

He said to me...“Why don’t you run...
I see you ain’t...got any gun”...
(All) He said to me, “Why don’t you run,
    I see you ain’t got any gun.”

Verse 4

I said to him...“That’s a good idea”...
So come on feet...let’s up and fleet...
(All) I said to him, “That’s a good idea,”
    So come on feet, let’s up and fleet.

Verse 5

And so I ran...away from there...
But right behind...me was that bear...
(All) And so I ran away from there,
    But right behind me was that bear.

Verse 6

Oh, what do I see...ahead of me...
A great big tree...Oh, glory be...
(All) Oh, what do I see ahead of me,
    A great big tree, Oh, glory be.

Verse 7

The lowest branch...was ten feet up...
I’d have to jump...and trust my luck...
(All) The lowest branch was ten feet up,
    I’d have to jump and trust my luck.

Verse 8

And so I jumped...into the air...
But I missed that branch...away up there...
(All) And so I jumped into the air,
    But I missed that branch away up
    there.

Verse 9

Now don’t you fret...and don't you
frown...
’Cause I caught that branch...on the
way back down...
(All) Now don’t you fret and don’t you
    frown,
    ’Cause I caught that branch on
    the way back down.

Verse 10

This is the end...There is no more...
Unless I see...that bear once more...
(All) This is the end; there is no more,
    Unless I see that bear once more.

In the Woods

Leader: Group:

Oh, in the woods, Oh, in the woods,

There was a tree, There was a tree,

The pret-ti-est lit-tle tree, The pret-ti-est lit-tle tree,

That you ev-er did see, That you ev-er did see.

All: *

The tree was in the hole and the hole was in the ground and the

green grass grew all a-round and a-round, And the

green grass grew all a-round.

*Repeat as many times as needed as
additional verses are added.

Verse 2

Now on that tree...
there was a branch...
The prettiest little branch...
that you ever did see...
The branch was on the tree,
And the tree was in the hole
And the hole was in the ground,
and the green grass grew etc...

Verse 3

Now on that branch...there was a
nest...

Verse 4

Now in that nest...there was an egg...

Verse 5

Now on that egg...there was a bird...

Verse 6

Now on that bird...there was a wing...

Verse 7

Now on that wing...there was a bug...

Verse 8

Now on that bug...there was a germ...

Verse 9

Now on that germ...there was a smile...

Kye, Kye, Kule *Ghanaian*

Leader: Kye kye, Ku - le.
Group: Kye kye, Ku - le.

Kye kye Ko - fi nsa. Kye kye Ko - fi nsa.

Ko - fi nsa lan - ga. Ko - fi nsa lan - ga.

Ka - ka shi lan - ga. Ka - ka shi lan - ga.

Kum a - den - de. Kum a - den - de.

All: Kum a - den - de. Hey!

Motions

As the leader introduces each phrase, he or she shows a motion.
The group repeats each phrase and imitates the motion.

Phrase 1: *Pat head four times.*

Phrase 2: *Tap shoulders four times while twisting from side to side.*

Phrase 3: *Tap on waist four times while twisting from side to side.*

Phrase 4: *Tap knees four times.*

Phrase 5: *Touch ankles on "Kum" and waist on "adende."*

Phrase 6: *Leader and group touch ankles and waist again, jump up, and shout, "Hey!"*

Translation

This song's lyrics have no specific meaning.

The Littlest Worm

Verse 2

He said to me... "Don't take a sip...
'Cause if you do... You'll really flip..."
(All) He said to me, "Don't take a sip.
　　　 'Cause if you do, You'll really flip."

Verse 3

I took a sip... And he went down...
Right through my pipes...
He must have drowned...
(All) I took a sip, And he went down
　　　 Right through my pipes.
　　　 He must have drowned.

Verse 4

And now he's gone...
And that's the end...
He was my pal... He was my friend...
(All) And now he's gone,
　　　 And that's the end.
　　　 He was my pal,
　　　 He was my friend.

Long John

My Aunt Came Back

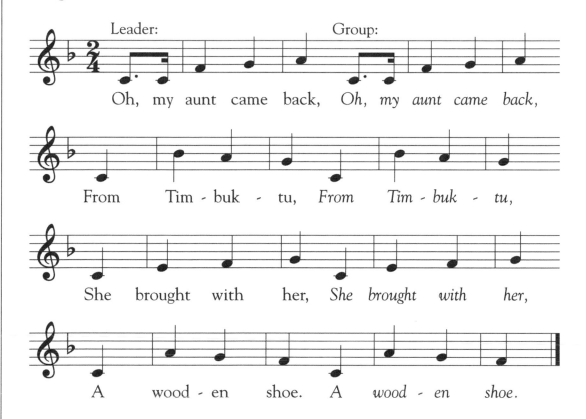

Leader: Oh, my aunt came back, Group: Oh, my aunt came back,

From Tim-buk-tu, From Tim-buk-tu,

She brought with her, She brought with her,

A wood-en shoe. A wood-en shoe.

Add motions with each verse

Verse 1

Tap foot.

Verse 2

Oh, my aunt came back...
From old Japan...
She brought with her...
A waving fan...

Also fan face with one hand.

Verse 3

...from old Algiers...
...a pair of shears...

Also "snip" using two fingers of the other hand.

Verse 4

...from Guadeloupe...
...a hulahoop...

Also rotate hips.

Verse 5

...from the county fair...
...a rocking chair...

Also rock back and forth.

Verse 6

...from the city zoo...
...a nut like YOU!...

Stop motions and point at group, they point at you.

My Name Is Michael

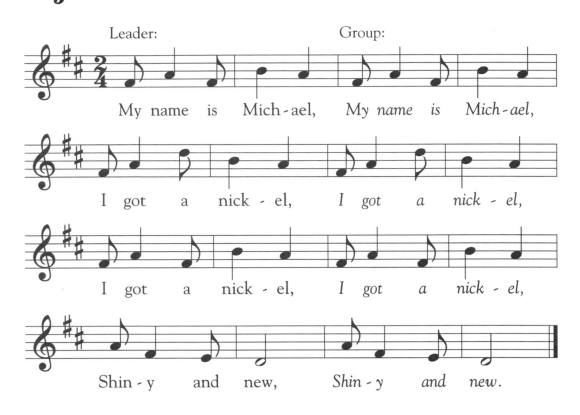

Leader: My name is Mich-ael,

Group: My name is Mich-ael,

I got a nick-el, I got a nick-el,

I got a nick-el, I got a nick-el,

Shin-y and new, Shin-y and new.

Verse 2

It's gonna buy me...
All kinds of candy...
It's gonna make me...
So very happy...

No More, My Lord

in Him A rest -

found *in* *Him* *A*

ing place, And He

rest - *ing* *place,* *And*

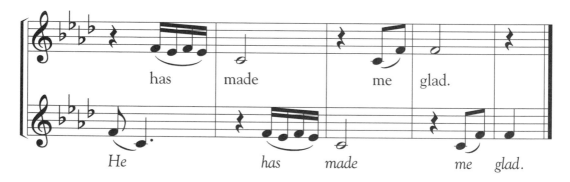

has made me glad.

He *has* *made* *me* *glad.*

Refrain

Verse 2

Jesus...the man...
I am look...ing for...
Can you tell...me where...
He's gone?

Refrain

Verse 3

Go down...go down...
Among...flower yard...
And perhaps....you may find...
Find Him there...

Refrain

No More Pie

Leader: Group:

Oh, My– Oh, My–

No more pie...
   Pie's too sweet...
I want a piece of meat...
   Meat's too red...
I want a piece of bread...
   Bread's too brown...
I think I'll go to town...
   Town's too far...
I think I'll take a car...
   Car won't go...
I fell and stubbed my toe...
   Toe gives me pain...
I think I'll take a train...
   Train had a wreck...
I fell and hurt my neck...
   Oh, my...
No more pie...

Old Texas

Leader: I'm goin' to leave old Tex - as

Group: *I'm goin' to leave*

now, They've got no use

old Tex - as now, *They've got no*

for the long - horn cow.

use *for the long - horn cow.*

Verse 2

They've plowed and fenced...my
  cattle range...
And the people there...are all so strange...

Verse 3

I'll take my horse...I'll take my rope...
And hit the trail...upon a lope...

Verse 4

Say, "adios"...to the Alamo...
And turn my head...toward Mexico...

Verse 5

I'll make my home...on the wide,
  wide range...
For the people there...are not so
  strange...

Verse 6

The hard, hard ground...shall be my
  bed...
And my saddle seat...shall hold my
  head...

Old John Henry

The Prettiest Girl

Leader: The pret-ti-est girl,
Group: The pret-ti-est girl,

I ev-er saw, I ev-er saw,

Was sip-pin' ci–, Was sip-pin' ci–,

der through a straw, der through a straw.

All: The pret-ti-est girl I ev-er saw,

was sip-pin' ci-der through a straw.

Verse 2

I asked that girl…"How do you draw…
That apple ci…der through a straw…"
(*All*) I asked that girl,
  "How do you draw
  That apple ci…
  der through a straw?"

Verse 3

She smiled at me…And said that I…
Might come up close…And give a try…
(*All*) She smiled at me
  And said that I
  Might come up close
  And give a try.

Verse 4

Then cheek to cheek…And jaw to jaw…
We sipped that ci…
der through that straw…
(*All*) Then cheek to cheek
  And jaw to jaw
  We sipped that ci-
  der through that straw.

Verse 5

And all at once…
That straw it slipped…
I sipped some ci…der from her lips…
(*All*) And all at once
  That straw it slipped.
  I sipped some ci…
  der from her lips.

Verse 6

And now I've got…A mother-in-law…
From sippin' ci…der through a straw…
(*All*) And now I've got
  A mother-in-law
  From sippin' ci…
  der through a straw.

Verse 7

Now sixteen kids…all call me "Pa"…
All sippin' ci…der through a straw…
(*All*) Now sixteen kids
  All call me "Pa";
  All sippin' ci…
  der through a straw.

Purple Light

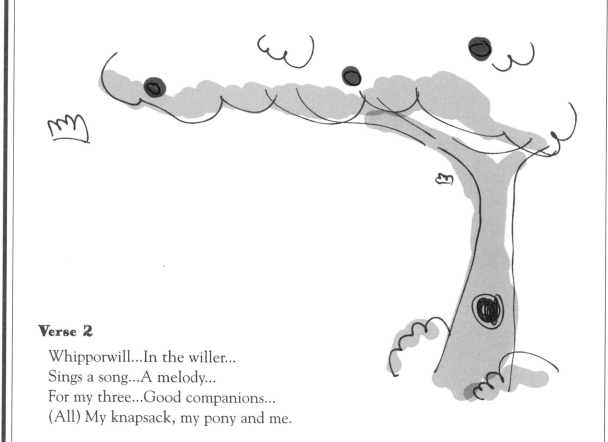

Verse 2

Whipporwill...In the willer...
Sings a song...A melody...
For my three...Good companions...
(All) My knapsack, my pony and me.

Verse 3

Gonna hang...My sombrero...
From the limb...Of a tree...
Over my three...Good companions...
(All) My knapsack, my pony and me.

Verse 4

No more cows...To be ropin'...
No more strays...Shall I see...
Just my three...Good companions...
(All) My knapsack, my pony and me.

Ricka Bamboo

Leader: Group:

Oh,   Rick-a bam-boo,   Oh,   Rick-a bam-boo,

What   do   I   see?   What   do   I   see?

It   is   a   bird,   It   is   a   bird,

High   in   a   tree,   High   in   a   tree.

It's   red   and   gold,   It's   red   and   gold,

And   pur - ple   too.   And   pur - ple   too.

That's why it's called, *That's why it's called,*

'Ole Rick-a bam-boo. *'Ole Rick-a bam-boo.*

This Old Hammer

Trail to Mexico

herd to Mex-i-co."

and fol-low my herd to Mex-i-co."

Verse 2

It was in the spring...time of the year....
That I took the trail...and drove those steers...
And it was a long....and a lonesome go...
To drive those steers...into Mexico...

Tongo *Polynesian*

Leader: Ton - go,_____ Group: Ton - go,_____

Chim-ney bye bye oh, *Chim-ney bye bye oh,*

Ton - go,_____ Ton - go,_____

Oom ba de kim bye oh, *Oom ba de kim bye oh,*

Ooh a - lay, *Ooh a - lay,*

Mah-le ka - ah lo way. *Mah-le ka - ah lo way.*

Translation

This is a traditional Polynesian canoe song. Though the song's lyrics have no specific meaning, the word *tongo* means "mangrove," which is a tree or shrub that grows along tropical saltwater coastlines.

Where, Oh Where

Leader: Where, oh, where,

Group: Where, oh, where,

The li - on,

The li - on,

One and one and one and one.

One and one and one and one.

Pass the peb - ble down,

Pass the peb - ble down.

Motions

*Children sit in a circle with their legs
crossed and their knees almost touching.
Each child has a pebble in front of him/her.
The following three motions should be
practiced ahead of time:*

1) Pick up the pebble with the right hand.

*2) Pass the pebble from the right hand to
the left hand.*

*3) Set the pebble down in front of the
person sitting to the left. This three beat
motion is especially fun with the two
beat meter of the song. (pick, pass, set,
pick, pass, set)*

Up Above My Head

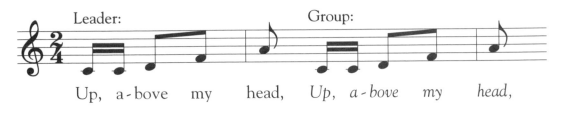

Up, a-bove my head, Up, a-bove my head,

There's mu-sic in the air, There's mu-sic in the air.

Up, a-bove my head, Up, a-bove my head,

There's mu-sic in the air, There's mu-sic in the air.

Up, a-bove my head, Up, a-bove my head,

There's mu-sic in the air, There's mu-sic in the air.

I real-ly do be-lieve, I real-ly do be-lieve,

It's a-head-in' some-where, It's a-head-in' some-where.

The Water Is Wide *Scottish*

You Can't Get to Heaven

Leader: Oh, you can't get to heav-en, Group: Oh, you can't get to heav-en,

On a pair of skates, On a pair of skates,

You'll skate right by, You'll skate right by,

Those pear - ly gates, Those pear - ly gates.

All: Oh, you can't get to hea - ven on a pair of

skates, You'll skate right by those pear - ly

gates. Oh, I ain't a gon - na grieve my

Refrain
Lord no more. Oh, I ain't a gon - na

grieve my Lord no more. Oh, I ain't a gon - na

grieve my Lord no more. Oh, I ain't a gon - na

grieve my Lord no more.

Verse 2

Oh, you can't get to heaven...
In a rocking chair...
'Cause the Lord don't want...
No lazy bones there...
Oh, you can't get to heaven in a rocking chair
'Cause the Lord don't want no lazy bones there;
Oh, I ain't gonna grieve my Lord no more.

Refrain

Verse 3

Oh, you can't get to heaven...In a limousine...
'Cause the Lord don't sell...No gasoline...
Oh, you can't get to heaven in a limousine
'Cause the Lord don't sell no gasoline;
Oh, I ain't gonna grieve my Lord no more.

Refrain

Verse 4

Oh, you can't get to heaven...In a motor car...
'Cause a motor car...Can't go that far...
Oh, you can't get to heaven in a motor car
'Cause a motor car can't go that far;
Oh, I ain't gonna grieve my Lord no more.

Refrain

Verse 5

Oh, you can't get to heaven...
In a birch canoe...
You'll need to paddle...
'Til you're black and blue...
Oh, you can't get to heaven in a birch canoe.
You'll need to paddle 'til you're black and blue;
Oh, I ain't gonna grieve my Lord no more.

Refrain

Verse 6

If you get to heaven...Before I do...
Just bore a hole...And pull me through...
If you get to heaven before I do,
Just bore a hole and pull me through;
Oh, I ain't gonna grieve my Lord no more.

Refrain

Verse 7

If I get to heaven...Before you do...
I'll plug that hole...
With shavings and glue...
If I get to heaven before you do,
I'll plug that hole with shavings and glue;
Oh, I ain't gonna grieve my Lord no more.

Refrain

Verse 8

Oh, the deacon went down...
In the cellar to pray...
He fell asleep...And he stayed all day...
Oh, the deacon went down in the cellar to pray.
He fell asleep and he stayed all day;
Oh, I ain't gonna grieve my Lord no more.

Refrain

Verse 9

"That's all there is...There ain't no more..."
Saint Peter said...As he closed the door...
"That's all there is; there ain't no more,"
Saint Peter said as he closed the door;
Oh, I ain't gonna grieve my Lord no more.

Refrain

Wise Old Owl

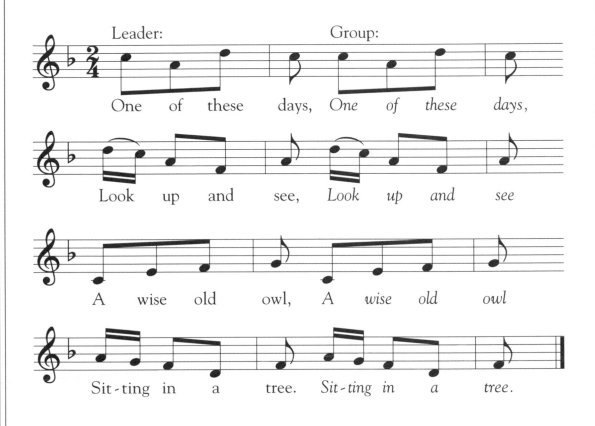

Leader: One of these days, Group: One of these days,
Look up and see, Look up and see
A wise old owl, A wise old owl
Sit-ting in a tree. Sit-ting in a tree.

Verse 2

He'll look at you...
And he'll look at me...
Those two big eyes...
They don't scare me...

Verse 3

One of these nights...
When rain drops fall...
He'll give a hoot...
He'll give a call...